NATURE LOVE
& WISDOM
A BREATH OF FRESH AIR
A FEEL OF LOVE
THE STRENGHT OF WISDOM, ALL IS DIVINE

To order additional copies of this book, contact:
Xlibris Corporation
1-888-795-4274
www.Xlibris.com
Orders@Xlibris.com

# Acknowledgment

In loving memory of my parents ,I would like to thank them for the important lessons and values they instilled in me at a very early age. I want to thank them for giving me the strength and inner peace that I needed to over come most of the struggles that our young men seem to crumble under in this troubled world.

I would also like to thank my brothers and sisters for believing in me. Thanks to my friends for the constructive criticism and for taking the time out to read my material. But above all, I would like to give honor to God for keeping me under his wings. Without him none of this would be possible. So, I just want to give him the praise .

Note:
I hope that everyone who reads this book will some how learn that it is through nature we are one. And it is by understanding nature we can understand who we are and who the creator is. For it is only the man of wisdom who will seek to respect the creator of nature, and hence respect himself and others.

# NATURE LOVE AND WISDOM

## Content

Nature:

Content

Love:

# NATURE AND YOU

Mother Nature, our heart and soul,
the mud the image of the whole;
the trees the plants, we all do need,
'cause the air we breathe that's all they bleed;
yet we destroy them in senseless deceit.

The rivers the lakes and the seas,
they all are there to refresh the breeze;
but from us all they take our fleet,
an achievement of disposal.
Nature is you, nature is me, whether you
are black or yellow, white or brown.
So let us all refresh each other, and live as a unit cell with all its organelles,
fighting together for survival.

So, do not try to destroy nature, for nature is you and nature is me;
'Cause Mother Nature gave birth to us all at the throne of creation,
hence nature we will always be.

## Be Thankful

The air we breathe the food we eat,
all these are so many; so be thankful.
The moonlight, the sunlight, the stars and the planets;
all are there for a purpose, so be thankful.

The streams, the trees, the rivers, the lakes and the oceans;
all are beautiful to you in their own way, so give thanks.

Nature in all its beauty is good for you, because you are nature.
Your body shows a figure, be it fat, small, short or tall;
so be thankful.
Be thankful for the morning you see,
be thankful for the night you sleep.
Be thankful for the children's love;
be thankful for the one that loves.
Though insignificant it may be,
Be thankful! Be thankful!

## Black is Beauty / Beauty is Black

Black is beauty, beauty is black,
without each other they have no duty,
In twain they shall reign forever.
The darkness that covers you is the tan which protects you from the rays of the sun.

So don't be ashamed and think you are dirty,
just be sure that you are mighty;
mighty in health, mighty in strength, mighty in mind
and body; mighty on earth and mighty in heaven.

Beauty began in heaven, and moved down to the
earth in Eden. So why can't you be proud?
Be proud that you have a duty;
a duty to show beauty, a duty to show blackness.
Inside, outside, and within that great mind,
let beauty be black, and black be beauty.

## Give thanks

Give thanks to nature for creating in you a perfect branch
from the seed that was sown within you at the feet of creation.
For sin is destined to deform thy child that comes from thee; to distort your
mind, and cause you to question the creator. So give thanks for that which you behold at birth.

Give thanks to nature for the branch that grows from you. For even after
birth Satan is still hunting to wither the soul.   Keep abreast with nature and
nature will take care of you. Yes, cherish nature the great healer.  For even
after the devil delivers his dreadful deed nature can heal.

## Nature's gift to us

The love we share is nature's gift to us
because in it, it's purity we've seen.
The smile it brings, the joy we live, nature's gift is so real.

The calmness, the happiness that is felt within is nature's gift of
healing love. The respect, the honesty and the integrity we share
is love in its entirety, nature's gift which completes us.

## A pleasure to behold

The rising of the sun in that cool early morning breeze, and
the sun lit sky on that mid afternoon is a wonder to behold.
The peaceful tranquil setting of the sun; and the starry sky with
the moon so bright, is another pleasure to behold.

Take some time to behold the nature around you and you will
find it is a pleasure to behold.  For within nature you will find
the peace and unity you are missing on your earthly journey.

The dancing of the trees in the gentle breeze and the sweet songs
of the humming birds within the leaves is a mystery of its own;
from the quiet stream within the valleys to the tides that rushes to
shore, we must know it is a pleasure to behold.

So I urge you to take some time to sniff a rose or two a day and
behold nature come what   may.  Take a little time from all the
hustle and bustle to see the bird soar in the wind and you might
just find it in you to do the same. For nature is a lesson and a
pleasure to behold.

## Flowers

*The flowers that bloom are scented, to capture the bees with its sweet perfume. The bees that suck on her must be in love with her completely. For the honey and nectar that flows from her must be sweet indeed.*

*The color that glows from her while she sits in the morning sun makes her attractive too. But I must tell you, yes, I must let you know, that the nectar is the sweetest attraction to her soul.*

*I COMPARE YOU TO THESE FLOWERS MY BELOVED*
*For beauty is within the heart of you, my love. Not the features that others behold. For within thee I have seen and learnt that you are a sweetly scented perfume.*

# Standing alone

As you walk alone within yourself,
with your thoughts centered upon your achievements;
you are standing alone.
Yes, as you go from day to day acquiring
all the riches of this world,
You are standing alone.
And as you build your mansions in every land and sea, while neglecting the poor to feed;
You are standing alone.

Yes you are standing alone because there
are children dying; someone who would gladly partake in the crumbs of your table. Oh yes you are standing alone if a helping hand you do not lend to the wounded son or daughter who has no one to turn to for some love and compassion. Yes, you are standing alone when you do not share the love that is in your heart to share. Yes, you are standing alone.

A little child has just passed on because of hunger my friend. There was not a table, there was not a chair, no there was nothing to eat, not even a bed in which to sleep. But you have just spent a million to buy yourself another car and another house, or maybe you have just given your concubine a second pay check to do her little feet. I call this standing alone, because it is all about you and not the suffering innocent ones of the world. Yes, it is all about you when with your eyes you have turned away, pretending you are not part of this world. You are standing alone.

You were blessed for a reason, and the reason I know is not for you to stand alone. But I know you were blessed to lend a soul a helping hand. I call that love, and love you must share when you have it, otherwise it will disappear. To you and the blessed people out there, do not stand alone but learn to share. Please give so that others may receive a little love, and peace, and food to eat because that is nature's gift to us.

## *Take heed of nature*

You slip your soiled air into my horizon you destroy my blue sky with your black dreadful nicotinic puffs and you wonder why my rain is not clean. You cut my trees, yes, you cut the hedge around my flowing streams and you wonder why I am drying. You liter all over me even in the deep blue sea and you wonder why I am not giving you clean  food to eat. Oh men of this world take heed of nature yes take heed of me, for vengeance will be sweet.

You are supposed to take care of me, that was the Master's plan, but with senseless deceit you tend to destroy my land. Yes you take from me my beauty and try to create your fake beauty. Yes you are laughing at me, littering all over me from the sky, to the rivers to the lakes and the sea, yes even from the mountains on high you destroy me. Oh men of this world take heed of nature, yes take heed of me, for vengeance will be bitter for thee.

I will blow my winds stronger than ever before, even in the calmness of the summer. Yes, I will send multiple tornadoes covering miles over your continent. I won't shy away even if you cry, for I have cried for many years. Oh yes, I will send the sun to burn your skin even in the winter seasons. I am just going to turn on you, you foolish men of this world, who cares nothing about me but your pocket of money. Take heed of nature yes take heed of me, for vengeance will be absolute for thee.

My ecosystem is disjointed and tarnished and you do not even wonder about me. What kind of heart do you have when you destroy me? Don't you know I am you and you are me? But I am just the mother who gave birth to thee? Rewire your brain and think again because you must stop destroying me senselessly. My sea I will cause to rise above thee, yes, my lakes I will make the winds rush to shore way beyond your walls and doors. Take heed of me, yes, take heed of nature, for vengeance will be mine one day.

## *To the dust:*

Way back then you came from me as you were formed by the one who created me. Yes, way back then the Master wet me, sapped me, made me hard again and formed you in His glory. He breathed within you and you became the whole, yes a living soul. Created through His glory and for His glory he said multiply and replenish the earth.

As you replenish me you tend to grow older. For you see, the younger souls your place they must take over. You live as the Lord desires and for seventy years you may live until you are retired.` But, I must say when it is all over, I am the winner, for to the dust you must return to await the master's second calling on that resurrection morning. If you lived like a holy son or daughter then I will set you free again, but if like the devil you lived, your soul I will keep to burn within forever.

# LOVE

Priceless
Here we are watching the children grow;
teaching them what they should know.
Yes, here we are watching the children glow,
giving them a better hope, a hope of a brighter tomorrow,
a hope of becoming the best they can be;
just let them know they are priceless.
They are priceless, they are priceless;
they can't be bought or sold.
They are priceless, they are priceless,
they are better than silver or gold.
Yes, they are priceless, priceless gifts of this world.
Here we are watching the children bloom,
We must teach them how to love one another;
Teach them how to stay together.
Yes, we must give them a world of peace,
a world of joy, a world of comfort, and most of all
a world of love.
They are priceless, they are priceless; they can't be bought or sold.
Yes, they are priceless they are priceless
they are better than silver or gold.
Yes, the children are priceless, priceless gifts of this world.

## My Beloved

Behold, you are my beloved!
Behold, you are fair my love!
You have dove's eyes behind your veil.
Your hair is like the feather of a dove upon which I keep my face;
Your teeth are like pearls in the glistering sun.
Your lips are like a strand of scarlet,
Your mouth is lovely and sexy.
Your temples behind your veil are like a piece of pomegranate.
Your two breasts are like two fawns,
twins of a gazelle, which feeds among the lilies.
You have ravished my heart, my lover, my spouse;
You have ravished my heart my love with one
Look in your eyes, with one lick of your neck.

Your lips O my honey, drip as the honeycomb;
Honey and milk are under your tongue;
You are the fragrance from the sweet rose,
You are a kiss from the rose my beloved.

## My Mom my only valentine

I wonder today who my Valentine could be,
Ah! I am sure, my friend should be.
But may be today it would be the most beautiful woman in the
world, my Mom my only valentine.

I wonder today, who my valentine could be,
someone who loves and cares for me;
oh! my mom the only one I think could be, my sweet,
sweet lovely valentine.

I wonder today, who my valentine could be,
Someone who teaches and loves me for me,
Oh my mom, yes my dearest friend,
I'll make my true valentine indeed.

I wonder today, who my valentine could be,
I think it will be a very special woman.
Someone that is helpful, truthful, nice and respectful;
And that is my mom, my only true valentine

# IF that's your woman

There you are young man,
Ohoo…in love with her you said.
There you are my friend,
hurting the one in your bed;
Calling her names,
Making her ashamed,
Putting her down
Over and over again;
Yes, over and over again.

And here you stand my friend,
calling yourself a man;
thinking it's cool,
breaking the rules of the meaning of true love;
calling her names,
Making her ashamed,
Putting her down
Over and over again;
Yes over and over again.

But let me tell you something young man….
If this is your woman,
You've got to treat her right,
If this is your baby;
You've got to lift her up,
If this is your lady,
When she hurts you must hurt to
If this is your soul mate,
When she cries you must cry to.
If this is your woman, treat her right.
If this is your woman, make her smile.
If this is your woman, let her shine
For the world to see and you will shine to my brother.
That's what love will do. If that's your woman treat her right.

## *The power of love in you*

The limits of life are heart breaking and tiring at times, confining
our mind, body and soul.  But the power of love that is within you
breaks free of all the obstacles making Prince and Princes of the whole.
For the power of love is the greatest source of our pure strength,
to overcome the evil of this dreadful world.

The limits of life could never defeat the power within you,
'cause the power within you is love;
yes, the power within you is love divine.
The love that suffers long and is kind,
It does not become puffed up or sublime.
The love that does not behave rudely;
It does not seek its own, is not provoked, and thinks no evil.
The love that does not rejoice in iniquity, but rejoices in
the truth within.
This love bears all things and endures all things.

The power of love never fails,
So when that power within you is love divine,
The limits of life are of no avail.

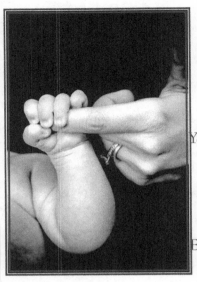

# You were there mamma

You were there all the time I needed you,
You were there to teach me throughout the years.
You were there all the time I asked of you.
Even in my desperate cries you were there.

But now the Master has called you home,
there is nothing I can do to take you back;
But I know the life you live will see you through,
'cause on the resurrection morning
you will be there once again.

You were there all the time I needed you,
You were always on your knees when my heart was aching
You were there to dry my tears
when my heart was hurting,
Mamma you were always there.

Yes you were there.
You were there.
Yes, mamma, you were there.
Even in my desperate cries you were there.

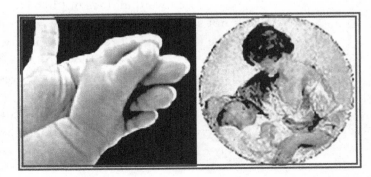

# From whence love came

From whence came true love, and to where does it go?
to ye who has a pure heart, and live for the world to know.
'Cause cheerful and joyful is the heart, the heart that always leaves
a smile to a broken one, no matter what color, race or creed.

You see, the sun will shine and share with all,
Be it rich or poor, black or white.
Then the moonlight comes and lovers go on,
down to the boardwalk hand in hand.

As they walk on the sands their footprints remain;
But the waves come ashore and take them away,
far into the oceans, and beyond the horizons, and into the heavens
from whence love came.

# Gorgeous mixture

You are a gorgeous mixture.
Oh my, the way you walk,
the way you wear your hair; the smile upon your glorious face.
Oh girl, you are just a beauty, describing
beauty in all it ways.

You are just a gorgeous mixture,
A gorgeous mixture, with beauty, elegance,
love, and joy written upon your face.
You are just a gorgeous mixture,
Yes, a gorgeous mixture.

Oh my, look at the way you dress,
It is amazingly wonderful.
Look at the way you keep yourself;
You glow in my sun, making my heart
stand still when ever I look upon your glorious face.

You are just a gorgeous mixture,
A gorgeous mixture, with beauty, elegance,
Love and grace written upon your face.
You are just a gorgeous mixture,
Yes, a gorgeous mixture in all your ways.

I have never seen beauty like this before,
A second in your arms will surely drive me wild.
You are surly the sexiest woman alive....
Oh girl, you are just a gorgeous mixture
of love, beauty, elegance and grace.

# *I just wanna say thanks*

I just want to say thanks,
for all that you have done for me.
Yes, my love I just want to say thanks,
for loving me the way that I am.

I just want to say thanks for being the rock on which I stand,
for holding my hands while we cross over the wild
running rivers of hate and strive of this crazy world outside.

Oh, oh my I just want to say thanks,
I just want to say thanks.

I just want to say thanks for being my woman.
Yes, my love I just want to say thanks
For bearing my sons;
through the pain of love, through the pain of joy,
you gave them to me, and for this I just want to say thanks

I just want to say thanks for making this house a home;
a beautiful place where I've found peace,
love and happiness of my own.
Oh my girl, I just want to say thanks.

I just want to say thanks I just want to say thanks.
For all that you have done for me,
and for all that you have given me.
My love, I just want to say thanks
For holding me when I was falling;
for sticking with me through thick and thin.
Ooooooooooooh…….(whisper) thanks my love
I just wanna say thanks.

## Just Imagine

Just imagine the world without you and me,
there won't be any sunshine or moonlight;
No, there won't be any stars or meteorites.
The milky-way will disappear into oblivion,
the heavens will no longer be.

Just imagine the world without you and me,
the rivers would change the course of direction.
For the sea would no longer be.
All the fishes in the sea would destine to fly
like the eagles in the sky.
Girl, this world would be in chaos you see;
there would be no melody to play a tune.

But imagine the world with you and me;
There will be the sun and the moon.
All the heavenly bodies will join in one accord,
and sing a melody to the bride and groom.

The roses will bloom and there will
be a melody to play you a tune.
The violin, the strings and the piano
will play softly as we hold close and move
across the dance floor of the glassy milky-way.
Just imagine !!!!!

## How beautiful

How beautiful are thy feet with shoe,
O prince's daughter!
The joints of the thighs are like jewels,
the work of the hands of cunning workman.
Thy navel is like a round goblet,
which wanteth not liquor:
thy belly is like a heap of wheat set about with lilies.
Thy two breasts are like two young roes that are twins.
Thy neck is as a tower of ivory;
thy eyes are like the fish pools in the deep blue sea.
How fair and how pleasant art thou, o my love, my delight.

# The picture on the wall

Ever since you've been gone
I have been hurting.
Everything in my world has turned dim.
Girl, everything is so blue.
But that picture is all I have of you,
And every time I look at it, it feels like
You are right there standing before me.

That picture on the wall,
That picture on the wall,
Ooh, ooh, that picture on the wall
is all I have of you.

Ever since you walked out that door,
The emptiness I feel is unbearable.
Oh my, it's killing me inside.

Girl there are times I just can't do the things I would like to do.
Sometimes I just wanna talk to you;
but all I have of you is that picture on the wall.

That picture on the wall.
That picture on the wall.
Ooh, ooh, that picture on the wall is all I have of you.

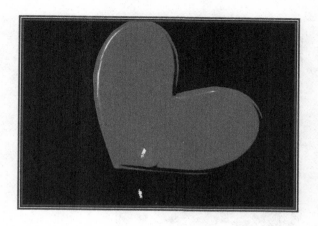

# Girl I Cry

Everyone looks at me and thinks that
I am a happy man;
but they don't know how much I cry inside, again and again.
No! they don't know how much I'm hurting inside with that unbearable pain.

Everyone looks at my smile, and think that I am a happy guy;
but they don't know the pain I feel inside.
No they don't know the tears I cry day after day.

If only I could open up my minds eye,
so the world could see my eternity;
they would never believe all the tears I cry.
No! They would never believe the Well of water that flows inside.
Oh no, they will never believe that I cry.

When I am alone I cry.
In the midst of the night I cry;
yes, my friend I cry,
so please don't let my gorgeous smiles fool you,
because I do cry
O yes!............ I cry.

# I am too shy

My heart yearns for love all day and all night.
But I am too shy to seek her, the one that would please
this lonely heart of mine.
I see her pass by everyday but I am just too shy to let
her know how much I feel for her.

Sometimes I wonder if it is me, or is it love that must
find me? Or must I get out there and seek what is gladly
mine......? It must be me, because I am just too shy to
call her name; I am just to shy to smile at her even
when she smiles at me. Even when she walks in my
direction I turn my head towards the tree which at
times is not even there. Man... I am just too shy.

Sometimes I would like to call out her name as she
passes by my door steps, but my lips would put on that
hydraulic brake and not a sound would be uttered.
I guess I am too shy...too shy to ask for love.

## The key to your heart

Give me the key to your heart
Let me come in and live within.
Give me the key to your heart let
Me come in and dine with thee. Let me
partake of your love divine let me be the
one you share that tender love with.

Give me the key to your heart and I
promise I won't slam your door.
Give me the key to your heart and I promise
I will stand guard even when you
are asleep at night. Give me the key to your
heart and I promise I won't let anyone in.
Oh yes, I will always be the one within.

# Tenderness

A tender touch is what I need from you a tender
smile is what I need to see upon your face. A tender
kiss is what I deserve from you a tender hug is what
I claim from you.

Love is tender; love is kind; love is everything but
crude. So if love is what we are sharing then what
love is then that I should receive; a little tenderness,
a little caressing and for sure, a few roses too.
Not bashing and bruising or kicking and slapping.
All I ask of you is a little tender loving. That is all I crave today.

When I see you coming home from work I want to
run into your arms not run away from you.
When I look at you I need to smile without fear of you.
When I am close to you, my heart should race;
not of fear my love but because of love for you,
that tender love we've always shared.
Just give me some tenderness. That's all I ask of you my love.

## Partake of me

*Partake of me my beloved partake of me my dear.*
*Partake of me every night. Partake of me because I am your wife.*
*Partake of me for I am the sweet viscose honey that was given to you.*
*Partake of me especially on the Sabbath day because I was created*
*for you just as it was created for you and me. Partake of me.*

# Lift me up

Lift me up my love and across the sky you will soar.
Lift me up my dear and upon the clouds we will ride.
Lift me up with words, lift me up with love,
lift me up with your care and the angels
will never shy of blessing you my dear.

If I be lifted up, you also shall be lifted up,
because we are one.  One in love and one in
unity from the day we were joined in holy matrimony.
Just lift me up and you shall
never fall from the heights where you are.
Lift me up my dear; lift me up among the
heavenly stars where we both belong.

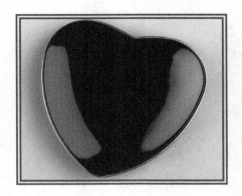

## *My heart I give to you*

*My heart I give to you because we were meant to be*
*My heart I give to you and freely it is meant to be*
*My heart I give to you as you have done the same*
*My heart your heart both are the twain.*

*This heart of mine is filled with love for you my dear*
*And I know your heart is filled with the same.*
*This heart, yes this heart I pour out on you with the*
*honey and kisses, is my greatest gift to you.*

*Upon my bed I will lay with you because my heart I*
*have given you.  Upon my thigh you may sit because*
*my warm heart I have given thee.  No one else will*
*ever get so close to me, because to you only I have*
*given this heart so real.*

*My dear, my beloved I just want to share all of me*
*with my love, who is forever near. Your eyes entice*
*me every time you stare at me. My heart quivers as*
*my mind is in thought of you, for you are always so*
*near with the touch of your tender hands.  My heart*
*my beloved you shall always share.*

## Let us say a prayer

Why do you always pray alone when from the same bed we arose?
Why do you always pray alone when we made ourselves a family many years ago?
Let us say a prayer together, yes let us say a prayer together,
and that will keep us together; that will surely keep us together.

Let us send our prayer to heaven with love and faith.
Through faith and love we can receive that joy of our heart's longing.
Let us pray this prayer together and together we will receive our blessings as a family. Let us pray:

Our Father! Whom art in Heaven, let this home be a place where you can live.
Let our minds and our heart be always centered on you.
Let us always find it in our hearts to forgive each other as we try to keep this home
a place where you will always be present. Let us live in love and unity so that our children
may see that God is our rock and our strength upon whom we must always
call on together as a family. Let the children of this home find peace and joy
within its walls so that as they grow up they will never find a better place
to be than this throng which we have created here upon this earth for them.
Let their minds be free from drugs, corruption and evil.
And most of all help us to be an example to them.
Let our prayer be answered this day;
MY SAVIOR SON OF THE LIVING GOD.
AMEN

## *What is your prayer?*

*What is the prayer that you breathe?*
*When on your way you are set to toil for the day?*
*Is your prayer one of haste?*
*Or is your prayer a prayer of thanks?*
*Or, is it a quick whisper that you don't even understand?*

*What is your prayer?*

*What is your prayer when you are on your knees? Or are you still asleep?*
*Or are you in thoughts of what you have not accomplished,*
*the day prior this? What is your prayer?*

*What is your prayer?  Is it my God give me wisdom*
*to train a young mind today,*
*or is Lord make me rich so that my enemies may ask of me?*
*What is your prayer…?  What is your prayer?*

*What is your prayer?*

*What is the prayer that you whisper when the little child in your care has suffered?*
*What is the prayer that you utter when your mind is wondering*
*on the sister or the brother that you just can't wait  to let have a piece of your mind,*
*because a few months ago someone stepped on your toe?  What is your prayer?*

*What is your prayer? If you can't live with your brother or sister; what is your prayer?*
*If your mother or father you can't ever forgive?*
*What is your prayer, If your prayer and your will are never of the Father's?*
*Well, If your prayer is like this or that, my, my I wonder what is the devil's prayer.*

# What do you love?

What do you love? Is it money, fame or fortune?
What do you love? Is it power, riches or glory?
What do you love? I hope it is love, joy and peace.
Yes, I hope it is the tranquil thrill of that morning breeze,
yes I hope it is that warmth within your heart that caresses that smile on your face.
Yes, I hope it is that gift of sharing, yes, that gift of giving to the ones who do not have.

What do you love? Is it the tear from a broken heart?
What do you love? Is it the blood of your enemy?
What do you love?  I hope it is the smile on the little ones face.
Yes, I hope it is the gift of the spirit to care for your fellow men.
Yes, I hope it is the desire to love and care and to treat all men equally.

### *Secrets of my heart:*

*You are the secret of my heart; you are the secret of my soul,*
*the one who gives me love and the one who makes me whole.*
*You are the secret of my heart you are the one that make this heart,*
*smiles aloft, such a beauty to behold.*

*People may look at me and wonder why I am so happy*
*but that love which we share my dear just makes me childlike again.*
*That secret love of our souls that no one can see,*
*is what we share and behold.*
*My beloved, your love is the secret of my heart.*

# What is your song?

Does the song that you sing put peace and tranquility in your heart?
Does the song that you sing leave your mind free of hate but full of love and peace for your fellowmen?
Is your first song in the morning one of cheerfulness,
or is it one that drives you to do and think of things that you do not normally feed that Godly mind with?
What is your song?

Is the song that you sing one of degrading words and lyrics?
Is that song in your mind one that tells you women are "no good for nothing?"
Is that song driving you away from reality,
eradicating the encrypted fact that you came from a woman?
What is your song my brother? What is your song?

Is your song uplifting to your brother?
Is it uplifting to your sisters?
Is it uplifting to everyone no matter what race color or creed?
What is your song?

## You pressure me

You pressure me to tell you I love you
You pressure me to say that our love is Devine.
But love should not be forced upon for love always knows its rightful place.

For love is natural and when it is present it will last a life time.
Yes, love is natural and when it is present the rays it dispels
will shine on the faces It draws together.

Yes love is natural and so it is given easily to the one that it attracts.
Love works wonders and ones heart it will always cause to skip a beat.
Love brings longevity when it is shared with the heart it's created for.
Yes love is all this and so much more.

So don't pressure me and let me think that there is love in our world
when my face you put wrinkles on each day.
No! Do not pressure me to say I love you when all you care
about is money and fame. No, please do not pressure me about love
when you can't even keep my home a peaceful place,
because all you ever do is force and fight.
Do not pressure me about loving you when all you care about
are only your friends, fine cars, and large homes.
Love does go beyond all these things……..way beyond this, so don't pressure me.

## At the end of the tunnel

Within the tunnel of misery and hate,
Your mind is destroyed with the thought of suicide;
Yes! Within the tunnel of the struggles of life,
You seem to blame everything on the other guy;
But to every tunnel there is an end
And at the end there is a light.

Within the tunnel there are shadows of light,
Bright enough to keep your hope alive;
So give thanks and praise to the father of grace, for at the end of
The tunnel there is a light.

Though your mind is in a whirlpool,
With the facts of poverty, strife and hate;
At the end of the tunnel there is a light,
still shining with a marvelous flame.

So, though you may be bombarded and dazed by the facts of life,
Entangled in poverty and disgrace,
Just keep holding on to the father of grace,
For at the end of the tunnel there is a light
shining from that heavenly place.

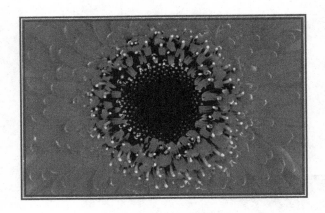

# The Strength of Wisdom

Wisdom is knowledge in action,
Which strengthens the wise more than all the
counselors of the city.
Wisdom makes the Wise man's face shine,
and changes its sternest,
For the strength of wisdom is great.

Wisdom allows the wise not to take to heart
everything people say, lest He hears the foolish
Say fallacious things about him.

Wisdom teaches you well,
And take the fool out of you
Which had cursed others who
destroyed your name in disgrace.

Wisdom is good with an inheritance, and profitable to
those who see the sun; for wisdom is a defense as money is a defense.
But the strength and excellence of knowledge is that wisdom gives life to those who have it.

# Turning point

There comes a time in our lives
When we must make a turn around;
Be you 10, 20, 30, 40 or 50,
because we can't always keep going down,
no we just can't keep doing wrong.

There comes a time in every ones life,
when we are down to the ground;
When our friends are no longer around.
Yes, when we have gotten too low down.
When it feels like there is nothing we can do
to make things better.
HEY!!!!!!!!!!
That is the time to turn around;
Yes, that is the time to turn around, turn around.
That is the turning point, the turning point,
To rise up to the best you can be.
This is your turning point.

Wake up my brother,
Wake up my sister,
You've got to stop doing wrong;
This is the time to turn around,
Please stop this going down.

Look up and see the stars above,
Look up and see the sun above.
Yes, now is the time to rise up from
Your lowest point and turn around;
This is your turning point.

## My Angel up in heaven

Today I called upon my Angel who is up in heaven somewhere;
to help me through this rough and lonely
road of making countless decisions.
The decisions I make each day will live with me come what may,
that's why I must ask for the wisdom from my angel
who will direct my living way.

The steps I make each day into the outside world,
may seem simple and naïve; but my angel I must ask for the guidance to go forth each day.
Without a call in the morning or at noon,
I feel like a fool if with my angel I fail to communicate.

In my natural self I feel nothing but despair when a prayer
I refused to send up in heaven somewhere. So, in my time of breathing this living air,
I promise never to skip a day of prayer.

## Heaven awaits you

As you go forth each day, sinning without a feeling of
guilt or shame...., heaven awaits you.
As the sins you commit become second nature to you,
heaven awaits you.
As the smiles on your face may grow,
as you reach your comfort zone in making the bad
seem good and wonderful, heaven awaits you.
Yes, heaven awaits you because it still cares about you.
Yes, heaven awaits you because it still wants to save you.
Oh yes, heaven still awaits you because the king still loves you.
As you go forth each day hurting the ones you meet on your way, heaven awaits you.
As you return from your daily duties and fail to forgive
The ones you have done wrong, heaven awaits you.
Yes, heaven awaits you because it still wants to teach you how to forgive and love.
Yes, heaven awaits you because the saviour's blood was shed for you.
Yes, heaven is waiting for a prayer from your secret throng.
So, do not fear what your past life may have been,
because heaven still awaits you.
Come just as you are. Heaven awaits you.

## My Mother's Prayer

In the still of the night and through
the cracks of our little country home I would
hear this little whisper. It was mamma praying.
And as I would listen closer, I would hear each one of
my siblings name rush up to heaven. Yes it was my
mamma praying. She was praying so that the devil
would not arm her children, yes she was praying for our protection.

Yes in the still of the night at just about the same time,
I would hear that sweet little whisper; yes it was mamma
praying again. And as I pressed my ears against the cracks of the fragile wood
of our little country hut I would hear that voice of thanks,
then a voice of praise then a voice of glory, then a voice of worship.
Yes that was my mamma praying, giving the Lord thanks,
worshipping the Lord, glorifying my God for hearing her sweet
little whisper in the still of the night.

Now we all have grown up and mamma has passed on.
I no longer have to press my head against the crack of our country
home to hear my mamma's prayer, as I can hear her voice in my head.
Yes, I can hear that sweet melodious voice which resound my name
on that heavenly throne throughout my growing years.
Though I can remember the tears we've brought to her eyes,
those prayers I will never forget. Because that is how I live my life today.
Yes through mammas' prayer.

In the still of the night I wake up to pray for the lord to protect
my little ones in this sinful world. Though they do not have the crack
of the little hut to listen through I know the lord will let them know
that I am praying too. It is only the faithful prayer that will keep them safe.

So I urge each and every mother and father to join in pray and send
a few whispers up to heaven so that heaven will protect our priceless gifts
of this world. And when mamma will pass this way again
I will let her know that all her prayers were heard.

## In the still of the night

In the still of the night as I set up to work under the candle light: they call it burning the midnight oil; I would wonder if there is anyone else burning the same oil. Oh yes there must be; they are those who have a dream to make life easier. Yes, those who have a mission to take their rightful place in this world.

In the still of the night when all you can hear are the sounds of the crickets, that's when you can find yourself working through the books. The twirling pages are sweet sounds to hear as knowledge and wisdom seep through the crevices of the cortex of your brain.

Sometimes it hurts. Sometimes dazed in sleep you bang your head against the table upon where you lay your head for a quick nap with your books. But you know that nothing comes easily, so you sit up again and then the following night; working vigorously because the time is coming when your knowledge is tested. Uh! You've made it through. The test was not terrible at all.

*Now you are making a good salary. Yes now you are living in a sweet home. Jealousy sets in from the friends who once laughed at you, and said that all you were worth was going to school. They have forgotten where you were in the still of the night. Yes they forgot the times when you were burning the midnight oil. They have forgotten that you saw nights turned into days and days into nights with just the pages of your books twirling before you. Yes they have forgotten.*

*But I would dare them to do the same and work for what they want out of this life. They are too scared to try. Yes they are too scared of failure so they won't even put a hand to the wheel. Hence the wheel will never turn. But if you dare, I challenge you to start burning the midnight oil and work through the still of the night and then you will see the joy that will come in the morning.*

*Hey, nothing comes easy. Unless you are ready to burn the midnight oil and break the still of the night you will always find yourself achieving mediocrity. If that is not your wish then put your hand and feet to the wheel and turn that life of yours around. Failure may come, but do not let that bring you down. Let that be your stepping stone to greater heights as you continue to break the still of the night under your candle light.*

## Who can do it but you?

In this selfish world outside you must do what you have to,
in order to make your life better for you,
because no one will do it for you.
Your life is yours and that you must take charge of.
Who can do it but you? No one, that's true.

If it means you must stand alone in pains and groans,
you've got to do what you must do to make
your life better for you.
Your life journey may be rough and long but in
your faith you must be strong. Even when you hit
the ground you must call for strength to carry on.

Who can do it for you? no one but you my friend.
In this world outside, everyone journeys on and so
self becomes the centre point. There you are lost in
the shuffle with no eyes upon you. So my friend,
this you must learn today,
that only you can make it better for you.

# Who are you?

*Are you a copy or are you an original? Are you the copy of someone or are you the original of you? The copy of someone will never bring the real person out of you so you had better drop that copy and pick up the real you.*

*You see, God created you so that he could work with you and not a copy of someone else. God created you differently so that he could make you make a difference wherever you are. So if you are a copy get rid of it now and pick up that real you.*

*Though scared and wounded you are from that old copy, the man from above will re-design you in His own way again. He just wants you to be you and not someone who has come through some form of greatness. That great person was an original not a copy. So if you want greatness, be an original.*

## Psalms37:23-24

*"The steps of a good man are ordered by the Lord:*
*and he delighted in His way.*
*Though he falls, he shall not be utterly cast down:*
*for the lord uphold him with His hand."*

## *Your worth*

Today you may be just an old iron lying in the
bushes with no worth at all. But if you take the
chance to let God rule that iron, immediately you
become centre of the pillar of the rich man's hall.

Today you may be just a worthless tea bag sitting on
the shelf, but why not let God give you your worth
by placing you in that hot water and draw the best out of you.

My friend you are worth something no matter who
you are, but you must allow the giver of your worth
to be the centre of unfolding who you are.
Let God show you your worth.

## We are different

We are different but still human, for nature will
never allow us to be the same. Some are short,
some are fat, some are tall, and some are slim.
Yes, we are different and to all respect must be given.

We are different but still human. We may be different in wisdom,
intelligence and acquired knowledge. Even in poverty,
greatness, riches, money or gold. But to all respect belongs.

We are different but still human.  Be it in political
aptitude or social attitude; in spiritual beliefs or
atheistic understanding. No matter how different we are,
we are still human and with respect as the key,
together we can live in peace and harmony

## What is your burden?

The burdens that you carry will determine what you
live for, but the greatest burden is to have none at
all. The burden that you live for have a price you must pay,
but I pray that you are paying for your own and not someone else's.


## What is your burden?

Is it to be the best you can be or is it to crumble with a little defeat?
What good is that burden if you can't set
your feet up once again to accomplish what you have started?
Let that goal, that dream, and determination be all
wrapped up in one and set sail again.
For what is life without a burden?

## Double minded men

Are you a double minded, or even triple or
quadruple-minded man? Then you are unstable in
all your ways; that's what the bible says.
You men must be stable in every way so you can
make sound decisive decisions.

A double minded man is likely to be a man who is
unstable on his feet, oh my! What trouble goes on in this mind?
A foot to the left and a foot to the right, there is no coordination?
Where is the body going to go as it wonders left or right?
Confusion sets in and so the body goes neither left nor right,
hence the whole being is at a stand still.

Double minded men need to rid of the second mind and
have the single mind work wonders by the will of the Father.
Let your decisions be sound and strong and for a perfect reason
you will be called great in the eyes of those who adore you.

# LAUGHTER

*Laughter! the medicine of the whole.*
*Laughter! the true medicine of the*
*mind body and soul which percolate*
*through the organelles of the cellular bowl.*
*Spend some time in laughter each day*
*for it is the door to the joy you behold.*
*Take some time to laugh my friend even*
*if in pain you may do so. For laughter will*
*keep the dead cells away and rejuvenate the soul.*
*Keep laughter on your agenda and your face will shine like pure gold.*

## Window of the heart

The windows to the heart are the eyes.
They declare all the hurt that you feel.
Yes, the windows of the heart are truly the eyes
Because they make known to me the thoughts you won't exchange.
The windows of the heart are the eyes.
They clearly show me the things that you hide,
deep inside the soul and mind.

# *Windows of my heart*

*The windows of my heart are four in numbers;*
*one of love, one of peace, one of joy and one of wisdom.*
*To you the keys I've given, for in sequence they*
*must operate to flow life through my veins.*
*So, if for a moment they separate, you I must blame.*
*The window of love is dear to me, because the*
*one I love majestically comforts me.*
*The window of peace gives tranquility, so when*
*the world is at war my heart is at peace.*
*The window of joy is the moment I spend with you*
*and the window of wisdom is the truth I share with you.*
*So the keys you hold in your hands are the master keys,*
*and should my windows be left unattended and broken,*
*you I must blame. You my love are the only*
*one who can cause me much pain*

## Give thanks......

If you can count your fingers in the morning give thanks
because you are alive. If you can count your toes in the
morning it means you can still see, so give thanks.
If you can hear a little child cry behind the curtains it means
you can still hear, so give thanks. If you can do all these
things at once then your brain is still wired, so give
thanks to the most high; give thanks and praise.

Do not take these things lightly because there are those
who wish for the blessings you take for granted.
Never forget to give thanks for the little things you can do,
because it's the little things which enable us to do the greater things.

## The heart of mankind

*Within the heart of mankind is hatred and sin.*
*Within the heart of mankind you find a haven for sin.*
*But if you look unto the heavenly King there you will find forgiveness for the wickedness within.*

*Within the heart of mankind there is jealousy and hate.*
*Within the heart of mankind is where strife congregates.*
*But if we look to that heavenly gate there we will find an antagonist for jealousy, strife and hate, eradicating the*
*natural tendency of this human kind to seek the blood of the weaker mind.*

# Happy is the woman

Happy is the woman who find herself a good man;
a man who works and a man who cares for the little ones;
a man who provides long term security for the family he loves so dearly.

Happy is that woman who finds herself an ambitious man.
A man who is sound in mind a man who do not flip in His ways,
nor  does he crumble at the feet of another woman's beauty.

Happy is the woman who finds a virtuous man;
a man of wisdom, knowledge, love and understanding;
a man who listens, but stands his grounds when he needs to.
But happier is the woman who allows that same man to be
the decision maker of her lovely home.

# Family

The family, the essence of a home
Family, they must come together at the heavenly throng.
The family in prayer is the family with wisdom,
envisioned to build a community.

Family, the essence of one home,
combined together to build a village from
one community to another.  So no matter what
we do, to stay together is a virtue

The family is the ingredient of the whole; the village,
the city, the country, the world. This world is just
an eternal bowl, with countless families originating
from the essence of the home.

So in love, unity and peace we must live because
we are just the centre of the whole. Yes,
part of one big family in this world.

# Quotes:

# 1
*Who can do it but you…..? Only you can make the best out of your life.*
*S.P*

# 2
*You can only see the rising of the sun if you are up early in the morning and you are facing to the east.*
*S.P*

*Quote# 3*
*The man who fails is the one who has taken a chance on greater things.  But the man who is afraid of failure is the one who will never achieve greatness.*
*S.P*

*Quote# 4*
*The best way to go on after a failure is to learn the lesson and forget the details.*

*Unknown*

*Quote# 5: No complaints after you've prayed*

*Do not pray for the rain if you are going to complain about the mud and sleet. Just go on with faith and enjoy the rain and the sunlight that you meet.  For your momentary dislikes may be the life long joy of someone else, because God has a greater number of blessings to share with each and every one of His children. So what ever comes your way work with it until the Master blesses you again.*
*S.P*

## Quote # 6
Take heed of the friends you keep. Thy true destiny may be defeated.
S.P

## Quote # 7
Never forget to show love to those you meet every day. It will bring joy to your heart, and who knows, you might have saved a life with the little that you did today.
S.P

## Quote # 8
Failure comes only when you have tried to accomplish something greater than where you are today, so when it comes, do not crumble beneath it: but rise above the scars and bruises, and step up higher using failure as that stepping stone to the top of the mountain where you belong.
S.P

## Quote # 9
Sex is the final touch on keeping your relationship, so have it as much as your health permits you.
S. P.

## Quote # 10
Love-making is the essence of how well you were created, so do it only in love.
S. P.

Quote# 11
*The flowing of the stream follows the easy course; and so life can be, if you spend a few moments to think of the things you do.*
S.P

Quote# 12
*Your body shows a figure whether it is fat, short, slim or tall; but wisdom lies within us all.*
S .P

Quote# 13
*Never forget to show love to one person everyday. It will bring joy to your heart.*
S.P

Quote# 14
*A healthy heart is the fun of sex but a weak heart may crumble beneath the joy of sex.*
S.P

Quote#15
*Your body shows a figure whether it is fat, short, slim or tall; but sex we must all enjoy because it was created for a purpose and that purpose is holy.*
S.P

Quote #16
Keep smiling…… it will keep the cells alive and prolong your life.
S.P

Quote# 17
Keep laughter on your agenda and your face will shine like pure gold.
S.P

Quote#18
Keep thy feet from the path of an evil friend, for they walk in the path of shedding their own blood.
S.P

Quote#19
Do not be wise in your own eyes for the wise man is known by the multitude that surrounds him.

Quote#20
Honorable is the man who seeks knowledge but greater still is the man who shares his knowledge.
S.P

Quote#21
The foolish lad despises instructions from the elders, but the son who listens to instruction is the one who will achieve greatness.

Quote#22
The heart of the wise teaches his mind great things, but the foolish man does not increase his learning.
S.P

Quote#23
A scoffer does not love one who corrects him; therefore he will never become a wise man.
Solomon

Quote #24
A man who is full of pride is heading for destruction, but a man of humility is building a path to greatness.
Solomon

Quote #25
Greed perverts the heart of an unrighteous man but the heart of the righteous is filled with love for his fellowmen.
S.P

Quote #26
The highway to freedom is to stay free from evil doings.
S.P

Quote #27
A man who is sound in mind will not quiver among a million fools.
S.P

Quote #28
Learn to appreciate the counsel of the elderly; for wisdom is entangled in every word that is uttered from their mouth if you listen closely.
S.P

Quote #29
He who has knowledge and understanding has a well filled with fresh water to distribute throughout a city that thirsts.

## You will always be my son

*You will always be my son I will be the strength to carry you on.*
*I will love you I will care for you; I will be there*
*no matter what trials may come your way.*
*I will stay with you my son I will show you how to walk in*
*this dreadful world out side.*
*You are the seed of my blood; therefore you will always be my son,*
*so my heart my love I will always share with you.*

*I know you never asked me to come into this world,*
*I know you never asked me for a perfect world.*
*But I must do my part to make your journey upon this earth heavenly.*
*Even though things may be tough at times, I just want you to know*
*I will always be there for you. I will be your shoulder to cry on*
*I will be the strength to carry you on. Yes, I will be the one to teach you*
*right from wrong cause you will always be my son.*